SCHOLASTIC

TRUE OR FALSE

Storms

BY MELVIN AND GILDA BERGER

Text copyright © 2009 by Melvin and Gilda Berger
All rights reserved. Published by Scholastic Inc., *Publishers since 1920.*
SCHOLASTIC and associated logos are trademarks and /or
registered trademarks of Scholastic Inc.

ISBN-13: 978-0-545-20202-2
ISBN-10: 0-545-20202-7

10 9 8 7 6 5 4 3 2 1   09 10 11 12 13

Printed in the U.S.A.   23
First printing, September 2009
Book design by Nancy Sabato

Storms come only in winter. **TRUE OR FALSE?**

FALSE! Storms occur every season of the year.

Storms form in huge, heavy clouds high above the earth. Tons of rain, snow, sleet, or hail drop from these clouds. Strong winds blow. Often, bolts of lightning flash across the sky, along with loud roars of thunder. Storms can cause lots of damage. But they also provide much of the world's water.

A storm cloud can drop millions of gallons (liters) of water in just one minute.

Storm clouds always look dark.

TRUE OR FALSE?

TRUE!

From the ground, storm clouds look dark to us. Storm clouds start when moist air rises high above the ground. It is very cold at this great height. The water vapor in the air changes into tiny drops of water. The droplets form clouds. The clouds look dark because sunlight cannot pass through. Heavy rain falls — and you have a rainstorm.

Raindrops in a rainstorm are ten times bigger than raindrops in a light drizzle.

A ring around
the moon
means a
rainstorm is
coming. TRUE
OR
FALSE?

TRUE! A ring around the MOON signals the approach of stormy weather.

You see the ring, or halo, because very high clouds often form ahead of a rainstorm. Inside these clouds, the droplets of water freeze into tiny bits, or crystals, of ice. When moonlight shines through the ice crystals, you see a ring around the moon.

As the old saying goes: "when there's a ring around the moon, rain or snow's coming soon."

Summer rainstorms in the tropics are called MONSOONS.

TRUE OR FALSE?

TRUE! MONSOONS bring heavy rain to tropical lands at the same time every year.

In summer, the sun heats the land more than it heats the sea. The hot air rises. Cool, moist air from over the ocean rushes in to take its place. These strong winds blow the moist sea air toward the land all summer long. Heavy rains fall, causing frequent floods. Many people build their houses on stilts to stay dry during the monsoons.

Summer monsoon end when the weather cools.

Ice storms develop from rainstorms.

TRUE OR FALSE?

TRUE! Ice storms occur as drops of rain freeze when they strike objects on Earth.

The raindrops cover streets and roads, trees and plants, buildings, and everything else with a coating of ice. Some people fall on the ice and hurt themselves. One terrible ice storm in 1951 killed more than twenty peopl and covered everything in eight states with an icy layer.

An ice storm car cover a 50-foot p tree with as much 5 tons (5.5 t) of i

Sleet is frozen rain.

TRUE OR FALSE?

TRUE! Sleet is frozen rain, or ice, that falls from high clouds.

Sleet starts as drops of rain inside the clouds. As they fall to earth, the raindrops freeze and become bits of ice, called sleet. The sleet makes loud clicking sounds as it slams into objects on the ground. In a heavy storm, sleet piles up on streets and roads, making walking and driving dangerous.

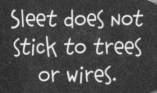

Sleet does not stick to trees or wires.

Lightning only shoots from clouds to Earth. **TRUE** OR **FALSE?**

FALSE! Lightning can shoot out in many directions.

Lightning forms inside huge, towering storm clouds. Here, powerful winds bump and rub millions of raindrops and ice particles against each other. This builds up a powerful charge of electricity. Suddenly a huge electric spark, called lightning, flashes across the sky. Lightning can shoot any way — down to Earth and up again, from one cloud to another, or within a cloud.

Lightning bolts light up the sky every second of every day.

Tall trees and buildings attract lightning.

TRUE OR FALSE?

TRUE! Lightning often strikes the tallest objects in its path.

A lightning bolt is drawn to objects that carry electricity down to the ground. Often these are tall buildings, power lines, telephone poles, or trees that stand alone or tower over other trees. Lightning that strikes a tree may split and burn it.

Lightning rods on top of buildings car electricity safely in the ground.

Lightning never strikes twice in the same place.

TRUE OR FALSE?

FALSE! Lightning may hit the same place many times.

The Empire State Building, for example, has been hit by lightning as many as twenty times in just a single storm. This skyscraper gets about one hundred strikes a year. People who work outdoors also can be struck more than once. One park ranger, Roy Sullivan, survived seven lightning strikes.

The most dangerous place t be in a lightning storm is under a tree.

Thunder always follows lightning. **TRUE OR FALSE?**

TRUE! Thunder is the result of lightning shooting across the sky.

As lightning passes through the air, it instantly heats the air around it. The lightning makes the air so hot that it explodes out. The exploding air makes the loud crack or roar of thunder that you hear. Since light travels much faster than sound, you always see the lightning before you hear the thunder.

When you see lightning and hear thunder at nearly the same time, the storm is very close.

Snowflakes are white.

TRUE OR FALSE?

FALSE! Snowflakes are colorless, like clear glass or ice.

But something happens when lots of snowflakes stick together. The snowflakes bounce back, or reflect, all colors of light. When all colors of light mix together, it looks white. So, lots of colorless snowflakes pile up and become white snow.

Every snowflake has six sides — and each snowflake is different.

A blizzard is a severe snowstorm.

TRUE! A blizzard is a violent snowstorm with heavy snowfall, low temperatures, and strong winds.

When warm, moist air meets very cold air, heavy snow may start to fall. If there are also powerful winds and freezing temperatures, the snowstorm is a blizzard.

In a blizzard, sno falls fast – about inches (5 cm) an ho

Blizzards last only a short time. **TRUE** OR **FALSE?**

FALSE! Blizzards can last anywhere from three hours to several days.

A blizzard lasting a few hours coats the streets, buildings, and cars with snow — and then moves away. But a long-lasting blizzard piles up lots of snow. The heavy snow, plus the cold and the wind, makes life very hard. Streets and roads are blocked. Schools, stores, and factories close. Power lines fall and many homes lose electricity. It often takes a few days to dig out.

Many blizzards come after a period of warmer weather in winter.

Hailstorms are winter storms.

TRUE OR FALSE?

FALSE! Most hailstorms in the United States occur during the spring, summer, or fall.

Strong winds inside dark rain clouds toss small frozen or semifrozen raindrops up and down, up and down. As they bounce around, additional layers of water freeze on the raindrops. Soon the balls of ice, called hail, are so heavy that they fall to Earth.

Kansas has more hailstorms than any other state.

Hailstones
are always
small.

TRUE
OR
FALSE?

FALSE! Hailstones can be as small as peas or as big as grapefruits.

Suppose you could slice open a hailstone. You would find a series of rings, like an onion. Each ring marks an up-and-down trip of the hailstone inside the storm cloud. The number of rings ranges from three to twenty-five. It's no wonder many hailstones are so big and heavy!

The largest hailstone fell in Kansas in 1970.

Hurricanes form over warm seas. **TRUE OR FALSE?**

TRUE! Hurricanes start when warm, wet air rises up from the ocean.

The rising air, filled with water vapor, forms huge clouds. Cold air rushes in beneath the clouds. The clouds swirl around faster and faster, like giant merry-go-rounds. Soon there are fierce winds blowing and heavy rains falling. It is the birth of a hurricane!

Hurricanes in the Northern Hemisphe[re] move from east t[o] west and curve towa[rd] the north.

Hurricanes can cause floods.

TRUE OR FALSE?

TRUE! Very strong hurricane winds often push ocean waters so high that they flood the land.

A wall of water caused by a hurricane is called a storm surge. It can be as high as a four-story building. The water floods the land, washing over everything in its path. The salt water damages buildings and covers farms, killing the crops. A storm surge can even push boats onto shore and carry them inland.

Storm surges and floo are the most dangero parts of hurricanes.

Tornadoes form on the ground. **TRUE** or **FALSE?**

FALSE! Tornadoes start in dark, heavy storm clouds.

Inside the clouds, layers of warm air meet much colder air. Strong winds start to blow. The winds spin around faster and faster. They form a twirling, twisting tornado. Tornado winds blow faster than any other winds on Earth. At the same time, the storm rushes forward with tremendous force and energy.

Tornadoes are called twister because of the swirling winds.

All tornadoes strike land.

TRUE OR FALSE?

FALSE! while most tornadoes do strike land, some never do.

Tornadoes that touch the ground move along rather short, narrow paths. The furious winds blow with deadly force. They smash buildings, level whole neighborhoods, and injure or kill many people as they roar along.

Tornadoes happen on every continent on Earth except Antarctica.

Tornadoes can pull up trees.

TRUE OR FALSE?

TRUE! The violent, twisting winds of a tornado often uproot trees and knock them over.

Tornadoes also have been known to overturn trains, buses, trucks, cars, and mobile homes. The greatest number of tornadoes in the world occurs in Tornado Alley, a stretch of land from Texas to Nebraska.

About 800 tornadoes occur every year in the United States.

Dust storms are like small tornadoes.

TRUE OR FALSE?

FALSE! Dust storms look a little like tornadoes, but they are actually whirlwinds and not as dangerous.

Dust-storm winds blow across the ground, picking up dust and dry soil. They form the dust and soil into giant walls of dirt. Most dust storms occur over deserts or places where no rain has fallen for a long time. Some small dust storms just raise narrow columns of dirt. They are called "dust devils."

A dust storm's wall of dirt can rea[ch] as high as a twenty[-] story building.

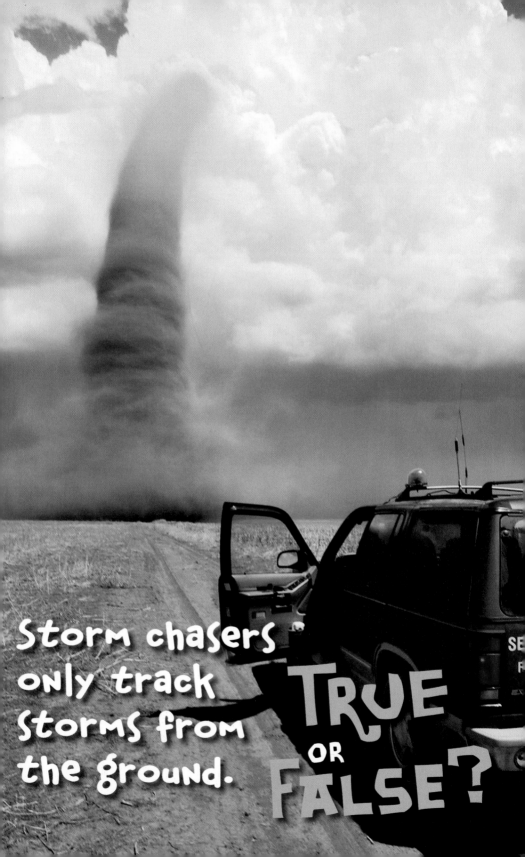

Storm chasers only track storms from the ground.

TRUE OR FALSE?

FALSE! Storm chasers work on the ground, but also go up in planes to track a storm.

Many use cameras and other instruments to film and measure a storm's speed, energy, and direction. Hurricane hunters fly into, around, or above hurricanes. The weather information that storm chasers collect helps us prepare for bad storms and be safe when one strikes.

Early warnings have reduced the number of deaths caused by storms.

Index